Life Changing Quotes

Senol Sahin, 07.10.2018

You waste so many weekdays waiting for the
weekend.

The master has failed more times than the novice
has even tried.

How lucky I am to have something that makes saying
goodbye so hard.

Comparison is the thief of joy.

We'd care a lot less about what others thought about us, if we realised how little they did.

The only time a man can be brave is when he is
afraid.

Chop your own wood and it will warm you twice.

Isn't it funny how day-by-day nothing changes, but
when you look back everything is different.

If the grass looks greener on the other side, you
probably forgot to water your own.

Victory favours neither the righteous nor the wicked.
It favours the prepared.

A man must suffer if he is to remake himself, for he is both the marble and the sculptor.

True nobility is not in being superior to your fellow
man, but in being superior to your former self.

A smooth sea never made a skilled sailor.

A raindrop never feels responsible for the flood.

Even the longest days are twenty-four hours.

If you are not hungry enough to eat an apple, you are
not really hungry.

A ship is always safest in the harbor, but that's not
what it was built for.

Work hard in silence, and let your success make the
noise.

If I have an apple and you have an apple, and we trade apples, then we both still have one apple. But if you have an idea and I have an idea, and we trade ideas, then we both have two ideas.

Do you want to be right or do you want to learn?

Be decisive. Right or Wrong, make a decision. The road of life is paved with flat squirrels that couldn't make a decision.

You're not in traffic, you are traffic.

Every saint has a past, and every sinner has a future.

Worrying means you suffer twice.

Don't ruin a Tuesday wishing it was Friday.

When you compare your insides to other people's
outsides, you always lose.

A wise man speaks because he has something to say. A fool speaks because he has to say something.

Don't make permanent decisions based on temporary feelings.

Never attribute to malice that which is adequately
explained by stupidity.

There's only two things in this life you can control:
your thoughts and your behaviour.

You can't control what happens, but you can control how you react to it, and that's what will be remembered.

Whatever you did to get yourself here, do the exact opposite to get yourself out.

You can let people walk all over you and they'll still
complain that your not lying flat enough.

There is a crack in everything. That's how the light gets in.

What is today but yesterday's tomorrow?

Beware the advice of successful people; they do not
seek company.

You must find the good ones, the bad ones will find
you.

We judge others by their actions,but we judge
ourselves by our intentions.

There are no big jobs or small jobs, only jobs that
need to be done right.

Twenty years from now you will be more
disappointed by the things you didn't do than by the
ones you did do. So throw off the bowlines. Sail away
from the safe harbor. Catch the trade winds in your
sails. Explore. Dream. Discover.

If the formula doesn't work, you change the formula.

One death a tragedy. A million a statistic.

Every person you meet is fighting a battle you know
nothing about. Be kind always.

To the world you may be one person; but to one
person you may be the world.

You can only shoot an arrow by pulling it back first.
So when life drags you back, it's preparing to launch
you forward. so just relax, focus and keep aiming.

No one can make you feel inferior without your permission.

Life is made of small moments like these.

You can never love people as much as you can miss
them.

You don't have to be the man you were five minutes
ago.

Stay afraid but do it anyway. What's important is the action. You don't have to wait to be confident. Just do it and eventually the confidence will follow.

If you wanted to be there, you would've.

If you keep lookin' back, you gon' trip going forward.

Inspiration is for amateurs, the rest of us just show up
and get to work.

This too shall pass.

To live is to suffer, to survive is to find some meaning
in the suffering.

Everything is okay in the end. If it's not okay, then it is
not the end.

When you do things right, people won't be sure
you've done anything at all.

A leader is best when people barely know he exists,
when his work is done, his aim fulfilled, they will say:
we did it ourselves.

Think of how stupid the average person is, then
realize half of them are stupider than that.

When you change the way you look at things, the
things you look at change.

Happiness is when what you think, what you say, and
what you do are in harmony.

You shouldn't keep others warm by setting yourself
on fire.

Treat others how you'd treat yourself.

A mistake repeated more than once is a decision.

You will only be embarrassed if you decide to be
embarrassed.

Parallel Lines have so much in common - it's a
shame they'll never meet.

The three things I cannot change are the past, the
truth and you.

I didn't come this far to only come this far.

The things you own end up owning you. It's only after
you lose everything that you're free to do anything.

If you always do what you've always done, you'll
always get what you've always gotten.

We do have a lot in common. Same eart, same air,
the same sky. Maybe if we looked at what's the same
instead of what's different, well, who knows.

You'll never learn anything from someone that agrees
with you.

If you cannot be weak, be strong!

The universe is a cruel, uncaring void. The key to being happy isn't a search for meaning. It's to just keep yourself busy with unimportant nonsense, and eventually, you'll be dead.

I wish there was a way to know you were in the good
old days before you've actually left them.

Being offended is a choice.

Fear is only as deep as the mind allows.

If you can't aim for peace, aim between the eyes.

Your life is happening right now and this is the only moment you can control. This is the only minute that really matters. If you are constantly dwelling on something that happened in the past or feeling anxious about the future, you are missing out on YOUR LIFE. Do what makes you happy in this moment and your life will be full.

If you're the smartest person in the room, you're in
the wrong room.

Suicide is usually a long term solution to short term problems.

Just remember, no matter how slow you go, you're
still lapping everybody on the couch.

Before I do something, I think to myself, would an
idiot do this? If they would, I do not.

It's not about you.

Truth is, everyone is going to hurt you, you just have
to find the ones worth suffering for.

Every day has the potential to be the greatest day of
your life.

Don't complain about something you aren't willing to
work to change.

The measure of a person is how they treat others that they are of no use to them.

It's better to be alone than in bad company.

Happiness starts at the edge of your comfort zone.

If you don't have time for it, it's not important to you.

He who cannot obey himself will be commanded.

Shine, while you live.

Stop looking out the window and start looking in the mirror.

Life is pain, highness. Anyone who says differently is
selling something.

Don't raise your voice, improve your argument.

Waking up early and going to gym is easier than not
liking what you see in the mirror.

A bowl is most useful when it is empty.

Give me six hours to chop down a tree and I will
spend the first four sharpening the axe.

Ever tried. Ever failed. No matter. Try Again. Fail again. Fail better.